I0187716

here is the house

the house nestles in

here is the dune

here is the sky

here is the ocean

here is the girl

here is the man

here is the woman

here is the bird

here is the wind

and here is the sand

the sand enters in

Leila Lees

Piripai

Piripai, between the mouth of the

Whakatane river and the open sea.

992
Press

99% Press,

an imprint of Lasavia Publishing Ltd.

Auckland, New Zealand

www.lasaviapublishing.com

Copyright ©Leila Lees, 2021

Cover Image, "Sand Dunes" Painted by Fay Lees, 1984

Design: Daniela Gast

Images of birds, shown in the chapter titles, are public domain works, created between 1844 and 1921. They were sourced from Wikimedia Commons.

This book is copyright. Apart from any fair dealing for the purpose of private study, research, criticism or reviews, as permitted under the Copyright Act, no part may be reproduced by any process without the permission of the publishers.

ISBN: 978-0-9951398-7-9

To the old naturalists and lovers of wild places

The birds are our first ancestors

Canary

Serinus canaria domestica

The girl enters her grandparents' house through the back door that is always open.

Through the back door is the wash house, big tubs, the agitator washing machine and the clothes basket. Enter this way and the girl comes to a small dark hallway where the telephone perches on a wrought iron and glass table. Turn to the right where the sun is already pushing through the kitchen door and enter the kitchen. Her grandmother is here, the sleeves of her pink cardigan are pushed up to her elbows, her fine white hair is mussed up as if she has jumped up quickly from a strange dream. Her grandfather is sharp-eyed and wiry. There is the smell of tobacco and garden sweat when the girl burrows into him.

There is crusty bread out of the oven, bananas, butter, marmalade and milk. The kettle is boiling. The oak wood table is covered by a linen tablecloth. The sunlight glows the wood and the cornflower blue cupboards smile. The yellow canary in its cage hops from one wooden perch to another and back again, hop, hop, hop, hop. The girl has brought in groundsel from the garden, the one weed her grandfather prizes. Groundsel for the canary. The girl pushes it through the cage bars. The canary temporarily stops hopping and pulls at the groundsel with its beak. Her grandfather lights up his pipe sitting on the red chair by the window. Her grandmother puts the teapot on the table.

There is a concertina vinyl door that opens into the sitting room. This is the sitting room. The light is filtered by the Venetian blinds; slanted lines of light and shadow fall across the copper coloured settee. It falls upon the glass cabinet, on the floral tea set, the Royal Doulton lady with the pointy shoes and the silver tea set. Missing the light is the brick fireplace, the toby jugs on the mantelpiece, the record player, the shelf of books. From the other room the canary bursts into a song, an aria that penetrates through the doorways and seeps into the dark rose-patterned carpet. Rich and melodious, the song breaks open its joyous heart. It is a song for the female finch that will never hear it, and then with a rich full stop, it ends.

Open the door opposite the front door, by the shelf of books, and there is the dark hallway again and down the end of the hallway is a bedroom. The magnolia tree riddles the light through the window that faces the road. The girl holds her arms oddly, like sleepy water that catches on a root impeding its liquid movement. This is her grandmother's bedroom. The girl watches the dressing table, the objects laid upon it. The finery of her grandmother's gloves, a smooth cream, the rounded buttons on the wrist, the fine wrist, the cut violets in the small crystal vase. Here is the pearl broach resting with delicate ease, and here the tight embroidered doilies protecting the mahogany. Here, an open drawer revealing white precise folded hankies. The girl looks back through the wide-open window, through fragments of white and pink voluminous blossom, broken perspectives, pieces of road as sharp as glass. The light skims the white tips of pink magnolia blossom, the colour of her grandmother's hair, that fall on the smooth green lawn.

This is the lawn that curves with the driveway bordered by white standard roses and pink stock. This is the jacaranda tree, the flowering cherry and the bent gum that towers above the road and the white metal letterbox. This is the road, this is the stopbank, this is the river.

Here is the long straight road that borders the fields of corn, green shoots on this spring morning. See how it follows and crosses the slow inky canal, and now parallel to the ocean it enters the dune. Here is the house that nestles in. The canary shifts its head skywards and opens its beak. The girl sees the trill enter the air, a silent rift. The man enters from the river and the woman through the remnants of dreams.

This is the ordinary life. The girl and the bird are part of the pattern in the weave of things. The girl cherishes the books on birds and herbs and a British book on bird watching. She treasures the smell of the small blue book *The Pickwick Papers* by Charles Dickens. She enjoys the feel of its fine pages and the small print. She re-reads *When Marnie was There* mixed with *The Book of Magic Animals*. Daily life under the peach trees, the absurdity of Mr Pickwick, the birds, the ghosts, the love. She writes *daily life* neatly in her diary. She reads that the riroriro, the grey warbler will destroy their nest, which they have been at great pains to complete, if they think they are being watched. She also reads how one ornithologist picks up a nesting pīwakawaka and turns it round so it's at the right angle for his camera. The girl mouths the word ornithologist and settles down on the blanket looking up through the blossom of the peaches to a weekend sky.

Grey Warbler

Riroriro

Gerygone igata

Here is the bird. Its song is large, its form a diminutive grey shape easily lost, a pixelated mix in the branches.

The girl wants to see it. She stretches tiptoe here, where the wind presses the grass, and here in the damp hollow. It doesn't occur to the girl that the bird is missing, until now, now invisible, visible only by its understorey song. She swallows its visible song as if it was ordinary. She sees it flitting down the branches where the line of kānuka trees accents the spaces; the girl's eyes fall into the unseen, between bent limbs, a shape like a small grey heart, vulnerable and resilient.

This is the song, a loud chortling warble, the notes high and varied. It creates a silence with its sound and she wonders what that space was like when it was empty, the space she never noticed.

The girl looks for the home of the enormous wild domestic song that reverberates through its fine bones. She comes across its nest when she is not looking. It is intricate, with spider's silk and thistledown, and moss the colour of water trembling, seeping from a crack in the rock. It is woven secure and is totally enclosed, lined with a profusion of feathers.

The girl watches the moonlit bones of the branches wrap their fingers into the weave of the nest. She is careful to be insignificant, for the art of bird watching is to let the bird pursue its daily life without knowledge of being watched. Here is the nest that lay in the song, wrapt by tatters of sleep. She lets the infinite cast its gaze through her eyes in the short passage between house and tree.

Here is a single feather hanging in the grass, in the yellowing grass, with the crackle of harsh light. Grey. Soft in the dry, dry heat, and the feather is ash in the shaft of light, the fine grey feather, hanging. She follows a trail of ants through the sand to its meagre form, to the penetrating small weight that fits in her palm. Frightening in its fragility, in its short passage of life.

She buries its tiny form in the sand amongst the millipedes and weevils.

She runs. These are her arms, these are her legs. She races the horizon back, through the dry grass, sharp seeds rattling.

Her home is outside the house but she does not know this. She turns the light off before she opens the door, the big pink moths tumbling empty in, stupid for the loss of light that drew them to bang against the window.

She sleeps with her bedroom door wide open, the ocean rumbling, a trumpet shell for an ear. Where her arm is, rests her head, the moon and the sea nudge the curtain, the long white curtain flutters. A star nestles amongst the hair in the nest. The nest starts to drift apart, silky threads of spider down and broken yellow paspalum stems.

The wind passes the girl over, quiet shifting the dust. On the floor, clothes stuck with bidibids and grass seed. Crouching in all the corners the air falling, the air, sleep sifting down.

14

Skylark,
Kaireka
Alauda arvensis

The morning dew splashes the grass where it tugs at the edge of the track and brushes wet against the girl's legs. Pōhuehu tangles over and into itself forming small bouncing bushes; divaricating and wild, it binds and bends the already wind humped kānuka and there it drops its leaves wearing a slight decaying aroma. In these hollows the sand is moist and smells of broken beetle wings mixed with kānuka leaves. This hiding place the girl lies back into, looking up into a circle of blue sky woven by kānuka and pōhuehu. The early, soft around the edges, morning concealing and merging with her edges, as if from her sleep she is still arriving.

In this place a liquid lilting song is pulled from the earth in one ecstatic line. She looks up to the downy underbelly of a skylark as it rises, fluttering its undiluted melody. The complex layer of sound moving quickly through trill and dance and rhythm. Each aspect a deliberate meeting of resonance. The air shifts to accommodate the weight of sound and then that too, stops.

There is an outline of space left, for the sound took up its space in the air.

There is stillness. The sun shifts a year. The current changes unperceptively. She crawls out from hiding, there are orange tips showing in the blades of grass and the sun angles in, displaying colours that trip with shadow.

Another skylark begins a zithering. A stretch of notes with tones that link spring with summer and sun becomes coincidental to the story. Thistle seed lifts straight up as if in concert to the skylark and the ripples on the sea shimmer in a contrast of warmth and cool blue.

There is no doubt in its continuous song. Neither sorrowful blunders, nor painful revelations. In her mind over and over the sensitivities to others are lost in the tympanic notes pitching her ear, as the skylark hovers still singing. The morning is up. The skylark loses height quickly and stops singing before reaching the ground. Porridge simmers, stirred with a pinch of salt. There's milk, the kettle is boiled and poured into the teapot, three teaspoons of tea, one for the pot. The woman looks out from the house drinking tea.

The girl finds her senses wake from inside and she is leaping over the grasses, over the tangled tripping stems of pōhuehu, down to the beach.

The dune runs undulating beneath her, soft falling in sand. To the edge of the dune the rough boxthorn leans in on an old fence line. Marram grass and pīngao, gold folding over the last soft sand before the sea, amongst the bunny grass, a rush of copper butterflies spiral off the sunlight.

Fantail,

Pīwakawaka

Rhipidura fuliginosa

The pīwakawaka appears. The daytime messenger, disclosing the small deaths, the things that fall in the cracks of the earth to never return. Its tail feathers flick and flash like camera shutters through the girl's mind: the old house by the creek, the grapefruit tree, the families in the street, Mrs Hyland, the pikelets, the willow tree, the trail of ants that wend their way through time.

The pīwakawaka is for now. It arrives like a butterfly, flitting and flicking, alighting, lifting off and alighting again. It materialises when the poroporo is planted, the queen of the nightshade family, its soft purple petals, exquisite, amongst its poisonous leaves. The man planted it with fondness for its gesture and for its reputation as a medicinal plant. He planted his medicine family of trees, the tutu, poroporo, kawakawa, tōtara, rangiora, patē and whau. He planted them under the kānuka and made a small sandy path. He placed a plank on two concrete blocks so he could watch the poroporo grow beside him and have a shady vista. From that moment pīwakawaka arrived. It talks with the man through a penetrating constant cheeping, a bright fearless looking, an aerobatic display and a beak full of insects. The man fills up an old copper urn with water.

The woman does not bother with this cool dark area, that holds its shadow in the heat of the day. The woman thinks with the wide sky and in-between there are things to do. The man takes the woman for a guided tour along the sandy path. He shows her each plant and the light sprinkles small leaf shadows on her arms. The woman observes the way the path curves, the placement of the plants so natural, as if they have always been there. Her laughter penetrates into the stagnant creases of shadow causing an invisible drunken shudder to go through leaf and stem and root. In the light behind, the toitoi becomes brighter and more upright.

The pīwakawaka lets forth a rippling movement of creaking cheeps, swiftly taking advantage of an insect convergence and where love leaves open the doorway in the peripheral hollow bone.

When the girl has athlete's foot, the man takes the garlic crusher from the kitchen crushing the patē leaves, trickling a dark green bitter juice to rub between her toes. In walking the long track up the Whakatane River on the edge of the Urewera, the girl develops a rash on her upper arms. The man picks tutu leaves to rub onto her arm. Poison is a medicine.

The girl furtively tip-toes into the territory of these plants, attracted by the wild hollow. The pīwakawaka tells every plant her whereabouts, no matter how quiet, how still and slow she moves. The poroporo sees inside of her. She is shy of its probing intensity, is repelled and transfixed by its finger-like leaves, its weeping dark berries. Kawakawa is more light-hearted, hanging its leaves to the east, stretching its dark red stems and with timing, divaricating. Patē is gentle yet inquisitive, with its fine serrated leaves, seven-fingered palms, hands that do not need to do but be, allowing the caress of the green light air. The tōtara is protective and prickly. It does not bend down, it shows her the strength of her heart by being upright. She passes the tutu bush and reaches the whau, its lightness a sweet relief. With a turn of her head she encounters the nonchalance and a touch of sassy in the castor oil plants who find their rich victorian-red voice, and hobnob with jet black nightshade on the other side of the path.

The pīwakawaka chirrups a squeaky song, flicking around her face, daring with its small sharp beak and bright eye, a wakeful threshold guardian amongst seduction. The poison plants become inky, rich and forbidden.

The girl once wrote a letter to her sister on a rangiora leaf. She gently pushed it through the official red post box slot, carefully written, stamp glued, address in neat capitals. The post office considered the fragility of this letter and put it in an envelope to preserve it with a small covering note. Now, as she passes the rangiora, she feels the past in her small life, the intensity of matter, of people gone. She yearns to wrap her heart in rangiora leaves and cool it in the waters and cool it in the waters.

She has a photo of the woman with her whole body lit up laughing. The woman is young, and laughing at the man who is taking the photo. Once, the woman smiled at the girl and the smile touched the girl to the ground and all the sounds became silent. The rangiora leaves are silent, white felt on the underside of its large pale green leaves.

The pīwakawaka comes into the house whilst the girl is sitting at the table placing stamps into old albums. Flitting, fluttering, and air jumping, repeating aerodynamics, it snaps at insects invisible. Around the girl and around until she is trapped, to-ing and fro-ing inside herself. She cannot cradle its warm gold beating chest, she is it and it is her, she looks for the doorway to the sky. The fantail's beak is fine and sharp, its eye is bright, perching a moment on the back of the chair, cocking its head to one side. I see you, I see you too. Then it is gone.

At night the pīwakawaka sleeps. The moon casts shadows in the hallways, wakeful night, the girl walks down the carpeted hallway. The leaves make patterns in the moonlight. A small brown moth disturbed, crawls up the window. The moon illuminates the edges of its dusty wings. It quivers on the wooden frame of the door. She pushes it open and with the moth, rushes into the sky.

Poroporo, patē, tutu. They speak the shadow language of the night, they grow on the periphery of the forest and the filtered light, and in the place of shadows. The girl, that is mingled in the other side, lingers, hidden from the light. The creamy soft underbellies of the rangiora leaves imbibe the moon. The inky lines in the poroporo become her veins as she fractures into the night. The endless movement of starlight remembers its pathway and all the sky is stretched with lines.

The man sleeps with the blankets swaddled around him as if he is in a cocoon about to be metamorphosed by the light of the searing night, unless he protects himself, wraps tight into sleep.

The woman, through years of blanket tugging, chooses to sleep in her own bed. The blankets stay intact, undisturbed, in repose, tucked in, arranged cleanly like gentle breathing.

The girl lies inside and under and through until the morning when she wakes curled in the grass outside her room. The woman opens the door to the blanket of darkness becoming immaterial. No one demands the woman's attention, only the vision of beauty; the way the morning cloud hangs on the horizon and the rhythm of cloud and colour transporting. She sits down in her own thoughts with a cup of tea, a smidgeon of milk and a half a teaspoon of sugar, looking through the sleep haze of the horizon. There is a sense of repose, a small row of rosemary flourishes blue aromatic flowers.

The girl watches. The light spreads across the page.

They both can't help but grin at the man, yawning, moaning, groaning, and singing sounds and stretching sounds like a vocal young tūī.

The pīwakawaka comes when the light is sharp. It expertly turns upon itself always precise in not touching the earth.

Morepork

Ruru

Ninox novaeseelandiae

Grief is buried carefully. A small failure inside an empty box. The box is lain on top of the ground and the sand is built up over it. That way, one could find it again. And open the box to smell the emptiness. Emptiness is a dry smell. It is best to open it at dusk when all the shadows are elongated and shapes are laid one on top of the other so it is hard to distinguish the shadows in a proper way. That is when grief can be opened and aired. Grief is normally hidden, as when all the adults go to Uncle Lloyd's funeral and the girl is left alone. She is underaged for grief. The aloneness is particularly accentuated so that she alone holds the unknown grief, the grief that is unspoken, the stifled grief wrapped in the embroidered handkerchief.

The box is wooden. She found it outside, under the eaves of the shed, tipped to one side, the hinges stiff. These hinges creak and grief creaks like bones. It is important, she knows, to hold the unknown grief, that is why the box is empty; unknown grief needs a space, a space inside, inside wood, inside sand, and land. Overtop she lays the empty caskets of the lupin seeds with their small precise pockets holding the memory of its black seeds. They spiral, dry, like a still helix. She places the wings of dead bees on top of the sand and the lupin caskets.

Grief does not have the bright summer yellow flowers, the blue petunias or the bright red geraniums. Grief is sharp, the wild barley grass seed, the dry arrow-like grains that fall away. There is dust in these sharp seeds. Grief is dust that covers the skin. Grief is the small grey moths that fall upon the interstices of the air. Grief is a still hand.

The box, the mound of sand, the husks, they must lie hidden in the hollows. That is where the ruru sits during the day. It just sits there. There is nothing she can do about it. It is wondrous with its liquid eyes, a constant inner stillness staring. She becomes peripheral to the bright life that eats the sweet seeds and drops its husks in the corners of the shadows. She edges into the shed where tunnel-web spiders secrete their white egg sacs amongst the thick webbing of their woven homes. They drop their exoskeleton litter on the peeling window sills. Through the dusty windows, in the dusk, the ruru moves silently into the growing night.

Mallard Duck

Anas Platyrhynchos

The mallard ducks dabble. They dive into the water with their tails up. The dabbling is a duck thing that happens in shallow water, mud and reeds. It involves duckweed, the curly weed that the girl puts in the bowl with the tadpoles she has collected. She feeds the tadpoles boiled lettuce and writes this carefully in her recipe book.

Her recipe book is a gift. The pages are cut, with different sections. Under guinea pigs, she writes; bran mash, mixed corn and rolled oats as a basic diet, all must be mixed with a little water or warm milk. She writes a list; cauliflower leaves, cabbage, lettuce, root vegetables, apples, clover, dandelion leaves, groundsel, fresh water. As an afterthought she writes; they also like a hard piece of fruit tree to chew on. The guinea pigs run up her sleeves and nestle under her jersey.

The girl sets the table for dinner. She puts down the linen placemats with the blue patterns, created with potato prints. She places down three mats with another long one in the centre. She uses the ordinary knives, forks and spoons. She places down the salt cellar and the pepper grinder. They all sit down together, the woman, the man and the girl. There are all the colours on their plates. The white potato, the orange carrots, the green silverbeet, cauliflower with a white sauce and for the woman and the girl, a lamb chop. The man is talking and the woman is laughing. The girl smiles, softening from the inside.

The girl is on her bike, when she finds them. Seven ducklings with soft yellow feathers and small dark markings, swimming in circles in a pool of dark water underneath the cattle stop. The girl lies down and reaches her hand down as far as she can reach. She manages to gently pluck them out and cup them in her hands. She places each one in her jersey to keep them warm, walking with her bike until she arrives home. They are already dying, their small bodies too cold, too hungry. She holds their small still lives, eyelids closing over and trembles.

Greenfinch

Chloris chloris

Exquisite beauty is painful. The breeze bends up the camouflaged paper wings of the yellow-brown moth amongst the shimmering shiver grass, membranous and translucent. The moth's vigour is precipitous, like a sudden breath before a soft trembling as if ice slid across the powder of its wings. Its vertical movements fall across the pale golden sheaths of the wild oat. The ache rests there in the sound the breeze makes as it ripples between the oxide colours of the dock bleeding in the sombre skies. Such transient vulnerable beauty is enough to topple the bravest hearts. A greenfinch lands to feed in the grass, balanced on the keel of the emergent leaf.

The girl is overcome by it. She cannot express it, the way the yellow merges with green so plain and fringed with the tassel of life. She is aware of attendance. The perception refracts off the already breaking down of the physical form. Her eyes attend in-between her heart beats. She becomes mute to the patterns on the wings, the interfolded softening of small parts. The greenfinch rocks upside down as the grass spins round, through the light weight of the bird. An artistry in plain things. She feels the prayer through her body, a bowing down to the dry rustling summer. Layers of prayer, pathways of prayer, the prayer that whorls through the earthy plant scent that wafts up from the ground. She wants the language of prayer, the patter, the pattern that could lead her to participate in this aching beauty.

It is the terrain that arrests the man. The formation of sand dunes, layers of sand, swept down, swept up, the tides, the wind, the river, rhythms of movement, erratic forces and the life that settles. All these parts play out, perfect and random. And the beauty of time, the man loves this and space and rest. Beauty is the slow time: a kaleidoscope of perception, geological time, the stars traversing the sky, the moon surfacing in the evening full and luminous, the sun setting the day, the day filtering out behind him, the fractal patterns of the divaricating forms of sand dune plants, reflecting surfaces, tilting to each other, looking, dreaming, visioning. He stands looking. Flocks of greenfinch fly up out of the great pattern of terrain, grass seed spinning out, as he trails his hands through the seeds and throws them out across the sloping hill like small gold shooting stars.

Pheasant

Phasianus colchicus

Hunkered in, amongst the sweet vernal grass, the close to the ground pheasant, a hen, still, shrouded by filtered light. Close to the ground, tunnelling under the foliage, the girl hidden, heart hidden, earth hidden into the earth hidden. Daylong entry, closed entry, open entry, the camouflaged old entry, a backward glance over there entry, arouses itself open, so that without knowing it the land opens like a shuddering sigh. The girl is daughter, sister to the land that kindles her sense of place.

The pheasant and the girl. The girl and the pheasant. Settling in, the land, open space, a covered way, an open sky. The pheasant, burnt sienna, burnt umber, yellow ochre, red and brown teardrop plumage, mottled and barred, her wings close to her body, nestling. The girl with the blue and white jersey, pieces of barley grass seed and bidibids caught in the woollen threads, fair hair, small wild carrot seeds their fine hairs catch onto her red cords, bare feet, she lies curled up, arm under her head, looking through grass, the seeds pricking the sky.

The pheasant has a watchful eye, turns her eggs carefully, a cautious attendance, stretches out a wing, a methodical preening, resettles, head down, an eye closed, only to open again. The girl scrapes back the sand, debris of leaf and tiny exoskeletons, millipede and moth wings, she imprints her hand neatly into the sand. A small orb-web spider swings from one blade of grass to another.

The man is home. He sits in a chair arriving into the late summer afternoon, his thoughts still interlacing behind him with the days that were, his heart tugging the line of himself, arriving into his eyes, into his chest, his heart, his feet with a sigh.

The woman doesn't join him. She walks through the sitting room, into the kitchen. She stands a moment contemplating the sky. The blue is faded, awash in the light. The horizon however is sharp. The light shows up the definition of form in such a way that it reflects back her own small frame. She settles into her bones and tastes the late summer mineral air, remembers what she has not lived and then forgets, as memory slips from her peripheral vision. Form becomes delineated. She lifts her consideration from her bones to the interface of her form, to the sense of space around her. She walks into her studio allowing her thoughts to consider her art.

And in the stillness, the earth becomes motionless. From the eerie quiet, a cock pheasant calls out, suddenly flushed out, an upwards crying spurt of flight, and another and another, whilst the hen stays alert and still. The earth rumbles. The girl sits up. The man moves to the door frame as does the woman observing the earthquake, one with curiosity and one with worry for the antique vase on the mantelpiece.

Welcome Swallow

Warou

Hirundo neoxena

The girl is pegging the washing on the large horizons. The clothes line stretches across the queue of kānuka to Orini canal and the township. It stretches taut above the edge of the plains before it knots through the wooden post at the end. Clothes dry quickly. The wind lifts the tea towels up and over the line, twisting the ends around the pegs. The girl was shown by her mother, who was shown by her mother, how to hang the washing out. Shirts were hung by the seams, tea towels shared a peg. This created symmetry.

Swallows flit up. Their expertise in air causes the domestic perching wooden pegs to become stilted. The swallows accidentally trip in the wind. The girl looks up, expectant. She is not sure why, perhaps it is the harrier hawk sweeping up from the paddock next door. The swallows let their tails momentarily hang loose before they dart and flick back towards the Orini canal where the midges hover in black bands.

She sidesteps the house. Voices drift along the windows. The woman is talking to one of the aunts.

"She can't live alone and he would never put her in a home."

"She would never forgive him anyway."

"I invited her to stay two nights at our place but she only stayed one night and then packed her bags. It's very hard on him."

"Maybe you have to be tough on her."

"But what say she drops dead? I'd never forgive myself. That's what happened to a friend of mine. She says she feels so guilty putting her into a home and she was so unhappy there."

There is the smell of muffins coming out of the oven. The teapot is being swirled with boiling water. The horizons spill into the grey cloud. The girl looks across the neighbouring fields; a blackbird and a hawk rise from the grass at the same time. She turns into the backdoor. The muffins are hot, the woman puts them out to cool. All the talking is leaping and bounding, sweeping up to the corners of the ceiling and sliding down the walls.

"The weather hasn't been too good this spring."

"I know the peas have gone all yellow."

"Edward kept following her everywhere. She'd been walking on the roof of the nurses home."

"Beautiful up there."

"She was depressed, you know."

"They put her in a room and gave her some drugs."

"The doctor didn't see her for a week."

"Did you know Tom had died?"

"She used to have a really messy house with piles of magazines so you couldn't move through the living room and the ironing board lying in the middle of the floor. Well, Jim went round there, and the place was all tidy."

"I just love that bird. Is it a wren?"

Tuan is here from Vietnam. The chess pieces are being

put down. The man is looking at the chess pieces and talking to the aunt. In the frozen time, the girl holds the plate of muffins, butter, jam and cream. The tea is ready to be poured. The sponge cake is having its final sprinkling of icing sugar – soft on the turquoise china plate. The good cups are out, matching their saucers with their delicate floral patterns, although Ethne, who has just arrived, prefers mugs.

The girl slips outside. She looks back at the canal where the swallows are beginning to congregate. The conversation behind her is muted. They are talking about whitebait.

The man walks out the back door. He shouts over his shoulder, "whitebait fritters for dinner," and grins. The old whitebait net hangs at the back of the shed. The man lifts it down. The aunts are following him and teasing him, looking for holes in the old net.

In minutes the bucket is found and passed to the girl who is already vanishing down the driveway, bare feet, with the bucket and the net. She is watching for the swallows, their constant darting, sweeping and whisking, in contrast to the Orini canal, travelling inky and slow between straight banks towards the river. The humped heaps of sand fall away to what was once wetland and is now farmland. Sluggish, the canal enters the Whakatane River bending a little as it opens out. It begins to weave between small scrubby islands that sit back from the stopbanks. Slowly the water widens and enters the mudflats.

Above, strands of cirrus clouds, ethereal, spread across the cerulean sky. They tell of rain due in a few days. The girl joins the other whitebaiters, standing around with their billy tea in enamel mugs. The whitebait flow up the river, the white nets lift them up, tipping the small transparencies into the buckets. The best time to watch the swallows is when the tide comes in. They move swiftly with grace, darting a constant aerial dance in the pursuit of the insects that are there, everywhere, above the water. The girl watches the constant flicking movement of the swallow above the river. The whitebaiters drift away. They have their catch. She stays longer before picking up her bucket of whitebait, drifting back along the track with the pole balanced on her shoulder and two swallows that dart ahead of her.

The swallows that can no longer migrate stay all year round.

California Quail

Callipepla californica

The sand builds up around the blade of grass, the stick, the spinifex, the log. The mounds grow, pīngao stretches, a fore dune forms. The obstacles that reduce the wind force are slowly forgotten. Above the high tide mark the sand starts to coalesce. Iceplant spills over the edge. In a dune, the sand can be dry moving or still and damp. There's a scent of old places, musty, where suddenly nature opens a cupboard door and lets out what's been hidden. That scent there, like what is forgotten, walks past.

The California quail know sand. They are on the level with it. They know grass and grass seed and small hollows. Sliding, unfixed and moving, wind will capture sand, swirling eddies that show up the wind's form, ceaseless. Like the quail, the girl knows sand, how it stings your bare arms, your legs and how you turn your back on it to protect your face. If she were to stand still like the driftwood, it, the wind would drop its burden against her.

The girl is lying in the dune watching small things hanging in the hollows amongst clumps of grass. She sees a sand scarab burrowing. As she sees it, it is seen, and paddling fast, it moves into the moving sand. The girl feels apprehensive for the scarab struggling through this puissant mountain of grey-white fine sand. The sand scarab with its large polished dark brown back burrows downwards into an endless desert. Under the driftwood or the roots of dune plants are the scarab larvae. It was these that her brothers dug out for her with some good rotten wood and a bit of sand to take to her teacher when she was six. Her teacher visibly shuddered and she was told to put it on an empty bench in the corner, furthest away from her desk. Her brothers, who knew this teacher of old, wanted to know exactly how she reacted. "Did she like the larvae?" they had asked, grinning.

The girl walks up to the house. The male quail, immediately alert, presses out his chest. His quills trembling, he sits up on the bank calling Chi-ca-go as if danger is about to fall from the sky. The quail chicks run after their mother in an eddying way. Vulnerable. The mother quail leads them nonchalantly through the back door of the house into the kitchen and out the front door. The quail chicks reel in the kitchen losing sight of the mother.

The girl crouches down a thoughtful distance away. There is always one. One small bundle of soft, tawny fluff with legs and a beak who is in danger of being left behind. If she touches it, the mother will reject it and so she tries to herd it in the right direction. "Go, go, go," she speaks through the interstices of mind, "go that way." Eventually the fluff gets a sense of where to go, lifts its downy feathers and flees headlong.

The quails' family hangout place in the early summer evening is where the driveway curves slightly near the top of the hill. The girl enjoys meandering slowly here, seeing how close she can get before the male with his striking black plume, rising erect, as if the whole of the chest is also erect that life is erect, begins to call. She would imagine trailing her finger around the precise white border encircling its black face. The female crouches motionless, camouflaged in coffee cream amongst the dry grass.

The girl keeps walking, pretending she can't see it. She is happy that the quail feels safe to her undiscerning eye. The girl plays with her peripheral vison, sensing the outline of the motionless quail until it becomes loud in contrast to the movement of everything surrounding it. The girl is going to talk to the man.

The man is digging a lake. A lake in the sand. There is a rhythm he gets into with the shovel, the way the blade peels into the sand, the way he lifts and throws the sand forming the banks of the lake. She watches the sprays of sand fling upwards and fall down. The girl talks and she wonders if the man can hear her, but it doesn't matter. She is talking to the sand and the shovel and the movement and the way the dune can hide one from the wind. It doesn't matter her words. Sand is like that, things can disappear into it.

The man can't hear any details. He hears the sound of the girl's voice. Some word infiltrates and sparks off another train of thought, thoughts of the past, of a conversation he was having the other day, and the neighbour and the pine trees, and the lake and how the lake will be and the water that will come and the reeds to plant and the trees to shade, and what happened on Sunday, and how to work, and how not to think, and something funny, and things he could sort out, and what to leave and things that were a mystery, and what to keep hidden there, still, in folds of the heart.

The girl has stopped talking. How long ago, he wonders, did she stop talking. He looks up. The girl is staring into a mound of sand. She has found huhu. The larvae of the long horn beetle and he is momentarily curious. The longhorn beetle lays its eggs under the bark in crevices. Then the larvae grow, tunnelling into the sapwood, the heartwood, excavating rich cavities, leaving behind an excrement called frass. Just before pupation, they journey to the surface of the wood and create a bed of the frass and shredded wood. At this stage of its journey the huhu is a great delicacy.

"Shall we go and cook it up?" he says. The man wonders why he is saying this. He hasn't eaten huhu before.

"Yes," she grins.

"I think frying in butter could be an interesting experiment, don't you think?"

"Ok."

The girl is happy for the experiment, happy for the momentary stopping of flying sand.

The man, who is a vegetarian, carefully gathers the soft creamy larvae in his hand and leads the way to a hot buttery frying pan.

Bittern

Matuku-hūrepo

Botaurus poiciloptilus

In the company of the reeds, the girl sees the bittern. It moves in a languid motion. It moves as if its body is liquid, repositioning itself by unfolding each leg sedulously, establishing a natural equilibrium at the edge of the lagoon. The moment the bittern becomes aware of the girl, it freezes. Motionless, it holds its beak skywards, as if its purpose is to become an eternal dive upwards. The girl imagines that at the end of its beak are stars, and beyond that a watery expanse. It is all a mirror. There is nothing but this, repeating and repeating endlessly above her.

The patterns on the water, the waterboatman, the small insects on the reeds, the flicking tail of the pūkeko, the constant sky eddy of the dragonfly, reckless clouds and a dropping sun, it all moves, except the bittern. In the stillness is the shimmering. In the shimmering the essence merges, there is no solidity; the feathers on the bittern have been woven into the reeds. Soon its tawny fern feathers dream themselves into the landscape.

The girl, however, has caught it out. She can see it, for the stationary bird creates a silent rent in the fabric. She holds to the truth in the illusion. The bittern holds its posture like a stiff prayer. Is it natural? Is it really there? She waits. The sky is getting shallow. She waits. The coots carry on their business, in small groups. She wants to share this absurdity with someone. This absurd bird who freezes like an arrow to the sky. With extraordinary synchronised movement both her and the bittern move at the same time, and then they both freeze as if they forgot the stanza they were playing together.

It is the girl who breaks the spell. She slips back, quietly, surreptitiously placing her feet back into her footprints, she wants this lagoon to be a secret.

It had taken nearly three hours of beach walking to find it, and as she leaves she observes acutely the large driftwood so that she can find it again.

It is late, she starts to run along the beach. The dotterel disturbed run piping backwards and forward.

The beach is repetitive, the same marram grass here as there, falling pīngao repeated like a series of mirrors, South African ice plant, petering slinters of yellow on the edges, soft tuffs of bunny grass, spinifex, drifts of wood that have been swept down by the river, sand building up, sand folding in, over and over, and in the distance the cliffs that edge the river glint in the late light, never getting closer.

Myna

Acridotheres tristis

The man is driving home. The myna, or one who loves a good argument, is loitering with his mates in the row of pine. They shift along, cajoling and shouting out above the corn stubble.

The pine, planted as windbreaks along the long straight road, meddles with the man's mystical vision of landscape. One myna struts off the road, adept in avoiding the car that is hurtling along. It struts quickly with the air that it is unhurried, that life is a cruise ship, and it moves with that insouciance until it has reached the road verge, before lifting off with its mates, calling raucously. The man is aware that the myna's flagrant communication is gatecrashing his goodwill. The mynas fly ahead, keeping in the man's line of vision, landing in the straggle of hawthorn trees with deliberate swagger. They are hardly settled before they fly up from these roosts to check over the lay of the land, and sidle down to the road.

The man has their measure.

The road turns and becomes unsealed. Crossing the Orini canal, the man follows the road through the sand dune. He stops at the old wooden gate, lifts it open as one of the hinges is broken, while half a dozen sheep look up at him from amongst the lupin. The second gate is easier and opens more readily, the driveway pressed with introduced pumice winds to the top of a small hill. The mynas scramble off the roof of the garage. Carousing, they flock upwards, and sweep around the house. One lands on the top of a bent kanuka, and as the man opens the car door, the myna calls out from its elevated position. A lengthy rowdy exposition, gurgling, chattering with a few bell notes placed in random unexpected points. All expressed in rapid succession in proximity to the man. The man feels churlish, a sudden strategic silence occurs, as the man and bird confront each other.

As the man turns away, the myna catapults up, chattering, and is joined by the others, chorusing together a night on the town or a spree where a few small birds might have been accidently flung out of nest, out of home.

The dune undulates with the wind. The kānuka grows in the lee and the spring wind gusts erratically breaking the kānuka branches. The defenceless pink, featherless birds fall to their death. The girl could do nothing for these oddly deformed small birds. She would close her eyes to the pink goosepimpled skin, the distorted beak, the blank eye. These broken birds seared her mind, imaginary birds fluttered all around her. The beaks were in her nose and in her mouth. They clung lifeless to her skin and she could not shed them, this un-fluttered life. The girl, who likes the myna, for they shared her curiosity, came to find that these small birds were mynas, the parent mynas in their first year failing to raise their chicks.

The girl reads that the myna came to New Zealand from India. They are related to the starling and have the ability to imitate the human voice. She imagines them in ornate cages being brought on a ship, talking back to a man in a black bowler hat. She imagines flocks of mynas above a field next to a dusty road in India, and a woman in a white dress telling the man in the bowler hat how she so detests birds in a cage. When the man in the bowler hat brings the bird in a cage to New Zealand, he remembers the woman in the white dress and he looks at the myna in the cage and he releases it. This pleased her, this picture of the man in the bowler hat and the myna.

The man, who loves a good argument, is looking forward to finding an opponent when it comes to politics. He is finding his father-in-law in fine fettle. Now how to catch him out with his thinking, how to push him a bit for those strong views to get traction. The girl pours tea into the good teacups with their matching saucers and the woman brings out the muffins, the jam and the cream sponge cake. The woman gives the man a hard look, which causes him to be momentarily discombobulated, grinning sheepishly he checks that he has remembered to put his shirt on from being in the garden.

In the heat of the day the girl watches the mynas sitting on the backs of the cattle picking off ticks, whilst the cattle, nonchalant of these birds, pause, looking out in the heat haze, flicking their ears and their tails. The mynas, she decides, are beautiful; the red oxide colour of their plumage, the striking patch of yellow below and behind their eyes, the white underbellies. They become acutely aware of her observation. She is suddenly shy in her exposure as they crack out their calls and one after another fly up like a gang, flaunting their patch.

The woman looks up and sees the mynas as the carnival piece in the landscape palette. Small and raucous, part nuisance and easily overlooked. It is how the sky is, the way the ocean merges and the fall-away land patterns that sometimes spill into the sky. This gives her the ability to allow the myna's broken holler of a call to submerge in the template of landscape.

The man struggles to ignore the myna, who rather than shouting out the territory, is having a particular specified word or two with the man. It is the time of day to contemplate the vista peacefully, to relax, look over the emerging English garden he is creating in the sand dune. The man sits on one of his wooden plank seats. He reaches under the seat and pulls out a bottle of beer. It's been a day of hot work. He looks in imagination of the future trees and the future lake and the future birds in the future lake. That dammed brassy interloper of a myna is trespassing into his transcendental landscape.

The myna, who does not seem to care, begins to encroach upon the man's disposition. It becomes the crux for a cantankerous temperament. The myna is a loitering gangster who ousts baby birds from the nest. It takes dastardly elation in pushing the precipitous edge of the sand dune over its constant precarious balance. The man's discrimination against the myna has begun to grow into an obsession. With unerring intensity the man considers the myna's demise. He comes to the decision that the way to be rid of the myna is to place a dead one on the roof of the house. This dead myna would be a warning to all the other mynas; then they would go elsewhere.

After some study, deliberation and mathematical

formula, he figures the best way to get a dead myna. It is to drive 100 miles an hour down Keepa Rd. In doing so there is a strong likelihood that those road-stalking birds would die. Unfortunately for the man, the mynas continue to adroitly elude their deaths.

Pied Stilt

Poaka
Himantopus leucocephalus

The pied stilts are written in the landscape in a scribbled calligraphy. The woman sees them like this. A graceful script in the marshy margins where the river is able to spread. The woman has driven the car as far as it can go on the unsealed road that leads to the river, and now, she walks a little way with the small folding stool and her basket with its oval wooden base. It contains a thermos of tea, a brown pencil case with a few watercolours, Payne's grey, burnt sienna, yellow ochre, rose madder, cerulean blue and lemon yellow. Inside the pencil case is a 2B pencil, a metal sharpener and three watercolour brushes. She has also placed in the basket a black metal fold-up palette, a viewing rectangle and a small glass jar with water. She holds her stool by the tips of her fingers with her sketchbook under her arm. Under her other arm a piece of watercolour paper stretched onto thin hard board balanced precariously with her basket. She finds a place where the river forgets it's a river as it merges waveringly into the reeds and the sky.

The pied stilts wade through the shallow waters, their long legs out of proportion to their small bodies, proceeding with amicable delicacy. The reeds shimmer, contrasting the black and white stark shapes of their small bodies. It is as if the woman can un-observe them, seeing them as outside of the landscape even though they are so precisely in it. At length the woman settles down to watch them feed in pairs, weaving amongst a watery backdrop. How careful they are, not to immerse their heads, like women who tentatively swim breaststroke keeping their hair dry and carefully arranged.

The woman places her sunglasses on and lets the tears finally leak down her face. She remembers once her grandmother pinching her cheeks and wiping her tears away with a small white hankie. She is uncertain where all these tears come from. She grew up learning to not cry and to be strong in the face of grief and now she is full of water.

She places her sketchbook on her lap and looks out at a landscape. The water has filled in all the spaces and left the sky and reeds and hills (that have lost their definition) to steady themselves in an oscillating vista. The pied stilt raises one foot above the surface of the water before placing it down, with graceful deliberation. The woman finds a steadiness within herself and smiles in response to the bird's conscious mincing gait. She guesses they catch the insect larvae with their fine black beaks.

She looks at the blank paper and picks up her pencil, translating the pattern of landscape. She lets the tears slip down her cheeks, wetting her neck, keeping her thoughts on the riddle of the forming artwork in her mind's eye. She pauses. She observes the vivid black eye of the pied stilt floating in a white expanse. All things become adrift. A whole lifetime empties out into the space between the object and the line. She grips what she knows.

With piercing impact, the pied stilt lets forth a high-pitched yipping call. It is answered further afield, and together the two pied stilts lift off, strong and swift, trailing their longs legs behind them.

Sooty Shearwater

Ardenna grisea

The man and the girl hover ineffectually near the woman before eventually departing. Adrift at first, their hearts skid restless until they focus into their various deployments, each in their own way putting down a small stone anchor through their activities. The woman, unaware that her hidden unhappiness had any effect, talks brightly on the telephone. The boats in the morning head west to get the crayfish off Rurima Rocks. They move steadily across the picturesque ocean, miniature dashes of colour. The shearwaters skim fast and low over the waves. Water, sky, island, coast, sea, salty water.

The girl, wearing her togs, flings the towel over her shoulder. She runs until she reaches the edge of the dune where the old boxthorn hedge stills grows along a bending fence line. She drops her towel, and digging her toes into the soft sand jumps from one foot to the other, down to the water's edge. The waves break close to the shore, there is a steep sloping bank of sand and the currents pull back, creating a surge of small waves that push against the incoming waves. She has to dive deep under each wave, getting past the dip, where the swells press down quickly, dumping all the welling surge into the sand. She is heading to where the breakers begin to form.

The shearwater glides without any apparent effort, interspersed with a few quick wing beats. The boat does its best to shear through the crests of the waves, rising up and banging down.

The girl rises up over the crest, to move her arms through the lacy pattern of the foam and feel the spindrift blow back to her as the wave crashes. The darker, dissolving areas between the white 'lace' are circles, like coins of different sizes strewn over a white cloth.

The water churns, eddies, curls, and swirls. The birds seem to be constantly moving, fluid groups, confidential to the heaving sea.

In the ocean a boil-up of fish surge to the surface. A frenzy of movement. Larger fish pursue smaller fish, propelling them upwards. The surface pings with a tumult of life. Terns arrive and the shearwaters appear, hundreds, intent on the rich feasting of life.

For the girl, getting back to shore is hazardous. It is almost impossible to not be dumped. The force rolls her, smashes her into the sand. She is grateful to feel the sand, that she negotiated the rip, that she found her feet on the ground. Winded, she struggles for breath.

In the evening, the boats head home to the east, crossing the treacherous bar before heading up the river to dock.

Kingfisher

Kōtare

Todiramphus sanctus

The girl walks down the grey, dusty road. The sky is angled by the sun that falls toward the mid-day. The small leaves of the boxthorn spill with road dust.

Collected in the brief shadow of the boxthorn, midges rise and hover in clouds, black smudges in the air. There is a deadness in the needless expanse of empty road. The sun comes to a stopping place as if in eternity the road is forever dusty and dry. The long sheds of the poultry farms bend and twist in the haze. She passes the Board Mill's dump to her left with the lupin scraggling against the fence line, already popping open their dry seed pods. The aroma of wild fennel mingles with the acrid acidity of the dump. The sun beats like a pulse in the sway of the road. The road has made a desert of the dune.

The road becomes a lost place. There is nothing to anchor. There is no life in the gravel. The girl feels stuck. There is no turning back. She is in the middle of her own traverse of the bleak road. Each step reflects the wire fence line and the somnambulant cattle. She brings her attention to the pond in the distance. A destination! there is a destination to a road. The pond rests behind a broken fence. There are frogs there but she has forgotten that frogs prefer the diurnal times of the day. She approaches it endlessly. A lone car passes by stirring up the dust, everything eddies around her, the dust, the leaning wooden posts of the fence, the spinning wire, closer now. The still water seems to rock without moving.

Where the water is, the land bends down into it. Cattle have wandered around it. There are a few bent reeds that hold themselves up in memory of wetland. What is left is the smell of black sluggish water. There is nothing but stagnation.

She looks straight up to see a kingfisher alighting on the powerline. It becomes utterly still in the harsh light. A sentry, perfectly poised. Its head is slightly bent forward looking intently at the ground, the whole of its body in a state of focus.

One part moves, its tail, flicking.

Australasian Gannet

Tākapu

Sula bassana serrator

The gannet dives. It happens with impetuous force. The dive is vertical, the wings bend back, the body forms an arrow compelled from above with a single purpose. The girl is in the water when the gannet comes down beside her. The water churns. Within seconds the gannet emerges, flapping out across the water with its long wings. The girl is intoxicated. She feels stabbed by bird. She dives deep, emerges, runs up to the house to talk, to tell someone about the gannet diving.

She becomes enthralled by the speed of their vertical dive. She reads how they can enter the water at 145 km per hour. There are inflatable air sacs in their breasts to cushion the impact, and they have no external nostrils. When they dive, they dive beneath the fish, coming up underneath with open bills, swallowing, all in a matter of seconds. She wonders at that 145 km per hour. She memorizes it. She takes notes. She wants to go as fast as that in a car to feel how the speed of that.

Her eldest brother suddenly arrives home with seven friends in tow, all male. Some sleep on the floor in the sitting room, some sleep in the back bedroom and some sleep in the library. The house fills up. Young men are in the kitchen cooking things she has never tasted before. They teach her card tricks and new card games. They talk late and sleep in and she has to creep around them in the morning. The woman wonders how long they might stay for. It wasn't something one asked directly. Perhaps hinted at in a passing conversation. Perhaps conversations around future plans.

Varying wind conditions change the appearance of water.

The girl watches the gannet. If she sees one circling high, catching the currents with a slow graceful tilt of the wings as it moves closer to the water, she would grab the binoculars from the sunroom's coffee table and run to the beach. She wants to see close up that premeditated arrow of flight.

The young men don't filter out one by one. They all go, everyone, altogether. The house empties overnight. Like young gannets they leave for Australia too. It can take six years for the gannets to come back to New Zealand waters. She reads this. It is inbuilt, this pattern of leaving. It is what you do at seventeen. She will do that too. The girl checks the spaces in the empty rooms, lying down on carpet, imagining the long flight the young gannet does over the tumultuous Tasman Sea.

Starling

Sturnus vulgaris

There is, the woman considers, a harmony exacted by the way one depicts the landscape through colour. The autumn hues of the dock, a drying red oxide tide, and the mingled soft greens with pink madder touches as the pōhuehu tangles the foreground, and that particular burnt umber undertow to the green, green haze of the boxthorn tips, overhung with the brooding grey sky and a merging ocean.

When the rain comes it brings out the birds. The rain is slow, trickling steadily, allowing the earth to exude the scent of millipedes mingling with the wet seeds of fennel, paspalum and wild carrot. The rain drips on the edge of the cement veranda, creating damp grey edges.

The man is in the library, his broken black-rimmed Woolworth glasses balanced unsteadily on the end of his nose. He is standing, holding a rolled-up nature magazine in his hand. He looks at the line of organic chemistry books in a dreaming, thinking way. The rain smatters the roses outside the window.

The starlings have been nesting in the eaves of the house on the west side. The girl sees their wisps of grass and straw hanging untidily as she dashes round the side of the house as if in her strides she can skip between the rain. Rain becomes noticeable when you are old. When you are young, wet and damp is felt in contrast, the beauty of coming back inside from the sparkle of rain, hot drink and the fire lit.

In the ngaio tree, a starling shakes itself, catching the girl's eye, flicking droplets of water in the shimmering rainbow of its wings.

The girl dashes by to find the hiding places, the dry spots under the crisscross of boxthorn, the bent kanuka, swept in the lee of the dune. The rain is visual, heightening subtle contrasts, enhancing the taste of the wild apples growing on the south side of the dune. She pauses briefly eating the apple looking out in the dripping landscape under the apple tree that has morphed out from the kanuka. She is running again crossing the old cattle tracks, skirting their huddled forms, the grass yellow, bent flat from the rain.

The day is a day of space, beauty unknown, beauty before beauty can be named. The day is soft and grey and wet and it shines up the colours that are only glimpsed and not seen. The discarded white curves of the apple core on the yellow grass, the black huddles of cattle in front of the dark seared macrocarpa, the no horizon line of sea and sky.

On the beach the driftwood lies about like scattered furniture that the river kings threw out, carved in a thousand images of beasts imagined. The sand is wet pocketed, the wood multi-layered, touches of gold and ores of silver. She walks along the bank pushing down the sand into the sea with her bare feet. Along, along and up and down the sand fills and falls. Her clothes drip and drag against her skin. She licks the water from her lips.

Colour edges and splashes, the yellow mist on the turret shell, the bright yellow flower of the ice plant and the eggshell blue of the linen flax. Eggshell blue, shimmering fragments, the pieces of shell, egg shell, sea shell, up, and up, the falling away cliff, the dragging spinifex, up and through wild humps of pōhuehu, leaping over the tripping weave of soft wiry stems. The rain steady now, in through the door, dripping wet.

Outside, the starlings are prattling. Groups fly up and fold like a broken wing heading towards the plains. One flies the other way, causing the others to talk more loudly. Pernickety over the wither which way, they turn back, briefly landing down on the grass, fussing. The woman looks past to see one fly up, a black rainbow with a smattering of stars. Up it lifts, its beauty unrecognized in its commonality. It leads the others, like scrabbling silhouettes, over the plain.

Pied Cormorant
Kāruhiruhi
Phalacrocorax varius

The cormorants roost in the macrocarpa, a disorderly perimeter on the south of the sandy peninsula. They go to bed early and wake late. They roost together amongst their construction of precipitous stick nests. The nesting time is over and the girl nestles into a collapsed macrocarpa, with its bent branches creating soft shady hollows. There is a pile of driftwood heaped against the old fence line. Sand-hoppers jump en masse amongst the heaped-up sand and driftwood.

The girl reveres these river-sea birds. She loves their hunt-alone dives, their emerging unexpectantly with waterlogged plumage. She hangs near where they roost together, observing shyly their reptilian faces, their blue eyes, their large black webbed feet, and when they line up preening on the damp compact sand that contours the river. She stands with them and she stands apart, watching the way the river eddies, forming deep pools in its constant shaping, re-shaping, a lip, a margin, in the river's widening momentum to the sea.

These are the long underwater fishing birds, their wings oily and wet and their purposeful bill, hook-tipped. The girl watches them dive and disappear in the water waiting for their coming to the surface – trying to predict where they will reappear. Sometimes she misses this emergence and they have already started to flap on the water before lifting above the small crests of the river, flying low and direct near the skin of the water.

She imagines them as creatures originating from when the sky slyly intermingled with river in the shadowy moonlit night. This love of two elements engendered the cormorant who is forever needing the air to caress its wings before it can swim like a fish in the river.

Now she sits adjacent to their ungainly forms as they line up on the sand, drying their wings, the offspring of the river. They stretch out their feathers. She stretches back her arms and pushes out her chest. Her hands are feathers. She stretches each feather finger out and bends her elbows as they bend their wings. The preening takes time, preening is essential. The man has told her, with keen spirit, that if they are disturbed and cannot dry their wings and preen them, then they might even die in the water. She is gripped by their potential death. Once her brother crept quietly up to one, and grabbed it from behind, and in that moment it died in his hands. She imagines how awful that might be. She stretches out her wings. The cormorants are oddly tame and insouciant.

The girl feels awkward, as if something came in the hidden night and touched her chest featherlike with ripples of water. In summer she now wears a soft top on her bare chest. She is as awkward as a branch let go of by the tree. She has learnt to speak one language but keeps the other hidden, curled up inside, submerged in river and sand. This allows some aspect of herself, of which she knows nothing, to stand remote, as witness, whilst around her things merge and come apart again.

Sometimes the girl walks with the man and the woman along the sandy peninsula. The woman watches the sky and the skid of the sky birds. She wonders at the way they take to air. Could she ever capture that freedom of flight on paper? The man happily botanises the river plants, bachelor's buttons, plantain, ranunculus and the little lilaeopsis with its small round tape-measure stems. They walk along the edge of the river to the mudflats, pausing to watch the cormorants. The girl enters into the river, diving down, holding her breath as much as possible to glimpse their paddling black feet.

Through the back way, they walk along the Orini canal with the tide in, pausing to watch mesmerising concentric circles in the still water. It is as if rain is arising from beneath the water. "Look, waterboatmen," the man whispers, as if his voice might ripple them out of the water, and she sees these water insects swim upside down. They really are boatmen, she thinks, as she sees their small front pairs of legs and their back legs, fringed with hairs held outstretched like small oars. Backswimmers, they create circles by carrying an air bubble in their abdomen and the oxygen from the water can diffuse into the bubble. "It's their breath," the man says, holding his own instinctively for a moment, "and every now and then they have to come to the surface to renew their depleted gas bubble."

This is where time becomes lost, watching small creatures in the soft hazy light.

The woman gets out her sketchbook.

White-faced heron
Matuku
Egretta novaehollandiae

The heron is long. Long necked, long billed, long legged, an elongated, listening, focused stillness. The girl can draw it with her finger in the air and one eye squinting. She draws it in one line, with hardly a bump for the head. Sometimes, she thinks, as she watches from the bank, slowing down to become mesmerised as the bird itself seems mesmerised by its prey, that there is no head, the eye is the beak drawn in one line. Everything is wired for length. Everything wired for the quick darting movement, the culmination of the listening, the seeing, the intent.

The heron is balance. The girl sees the balance like a point of entry, like the seesaw pausing at the fulcrum. Here is the entry. Amongst the anchored beauty her breath steams through space. The heron does mist, the morning mist on the river, the morning mist that hides the edges that brings things in close and softens the way. Everything has space. The heron tucks one leg into its body.

The heron is peace. It samples the food as it passes in placid watery pools. The heron becomes part of the tidal edge places and the slow-moving water places. It is a dimension of rock pools, the edge of the river, the wetlands in the dunes, the wetlands where the land sinks around the bow-shaped river, behind the stopbanks, where the reeds poke between the grass, and where all the canals and drains and the will of the farmer cannot keep the water out of the paddocks. The water spills upwards settling in pools. Cockabullies, tadpoles, frogs, waterboatmen, spiders, molluscs become sweet morsels.

The heron is invisible. Soft blue-grey, its feathers loosen the edges so that it seems to merge with the foreground. The girl watches this magical ability to become one with the patterns around it, somehow sending them adrift, floating in such a way that the air is watery and reflective. She is adrift as her internal and external world flap up against each other. She spends more time on the river bank walking one way and the river flowing the other.

The heron is dream. When it lands as it does sometimes, in the playing field, it folds its wings in gracefully. This allows the girl freedom in the dreaming eye. The heron exists beyond the classroom, beyond the petty chalk on the blackboard, and beyond the mean grizzled face of the teacher. He is a man held fast to his own boy bully. His eyes focus grimly on that which might be beyond control, even untouchable, as remote as a single soft, steel-blue feather on the outstretched wing of the heron as it lifts its leg and preens its wing with its foot. The girl watches. She slips down an invisible pathway, and all the shouting cannot reach her inner already dancing on the scooped back, in the ruffled feathers, as the heron strides through the wet grass bending its neck as if reflecting the lost bow bend of the river.

The children are gathered tightly. The teachers are striding up and down. It's sports day, nobody is moving.

Every child has to be wearing the right outfit, and every child is held prisoner to the cadence of the man that holds his superiority in small fat fists. He is shouting at the girl and is striding towards her whilst all the school is in silent witness. Unable to move, she wonders what language he is speaking, as the heron lifts up off the ground with its broad wings flapping slowly, deliberately. She sees its neck contracted, its legs dangling untidily, and then in all its grace it lets its harsh croak rend the air, waking her so she can comprehend the fat bully man standing above her.

Fernbird

Mātātā

Megalurus punctatus

Strands of the autumn orb spiders' web stretch from the fine tips of grass and reed. A single line balanced so finely that the sun catches it in the early morning. The spiders, jewel-like, nephrite green and opal. The girl rushes into the outside, before the day can decide itself. Now she stands, uncertainly, seeing the broken threads of web, and how all her movement has cut through them. She crawls under and around the intricate threading. This is the window of seeing, when the light is soft and fine. Very soon each thread becomes invisible. If she runs, she can get down to the marsh and watch the spiders in the ribbonwood. There, red damselflies hover above the water, the canal runs into the marsh and she can lean down and watch small fish slip through the dark water.

All at once she feels oddly deflated. The sun has shifted and all the webs are invisible. Her limbs seem to move from a distance. The road is already preparing for the dust, and there is the indefatigable loss of the gloaming as the light asserts itself. The girl walks backwards letting her thoughts trail, seeing how far she can go without looking behind. She deliberately walks backwards into the fence line as she is already narrating a story about a mouse and a fence and then she is running zigzag along the road, words jumbling out onto the horizon. And stops abruptly, enjoying the fact that humans are slumbering.

She walks until the road reaches a wooden gate, beyond is a rutted track. The canal is moving into the river where it becomes tidal with the ocean pressing in.

She hears a piercing bird call. It stills her. She waits as if she were a web ladder, invisible in the sun. She waits with the midges spinning vortexes, she waits looking as if she is looking the other way, and she finally glimpses it – mātātā, fern bird.

In awe, she becomes not here *and* here. Mātātā is running like a soft feathery mouse through the twiggy, thorny shrubs, the sharp cutty grass, the carex, the mānuka and the reeds. She glimpses silky markings and a long feathery tail.

It vanishes as quickly as it appears. The girl wonders at its existence. She is entranced, she is immobile, the raupō, the fractured dry mud, the stiff gorse, she is the watching ribbonwood, watching through the scrub, the sedges, the reeds and the mud. The mud is sometimes oily and sometimes cracked and dry. The tide is half-way and so still glistening. The reeds tremble. She becomes aware that mātātā is the cause of the trembling reeds. Its light body quivering them. She watches the reeds move as it weaves in and out, and through them. She can tell where it has been but she can't see it.

It shifts through the margins and then is gone. It falls into the unoccupied, into the rift, into an empty silence. It disappears into its own existence.

Life is now hungry. The road is dull and weighty. It's rough on the feet. She runs along the edge, slips through the next door paddock and makes a beeline to the middle gate.

Maybe she could eat cheese on toast, tea and marmalade on toast or even better still, sweetcorn fritters with sprinklings of salt. She slams the door as she enters the house, and no one is awake.

Waxeye
Tauhou
Zosterops lateralis

The waxeye dies. Its accidental death is the result of a jolt, having slammed into the window. It lies on the cement veranda in a small heap of soft yellow-green feathers. The rest of the flock sit in the ngaio tree that borders the lawn. The waxeyes are congregating in their small winter flocks. The girl has observed them in flocks with a single fantail combing the peach orchard. They moved up to spend time amongst the kānuka and the kawakawa, and then found the seeds of the karamu before settling in the ngaio tree. The ngaio trunks bend smoothly together like a pair of tango dancers, and the waxeyes perch in all layers of the tree. The tree presses towards the northeast where a sandy bank protects it from most of the wind, except its upper branches which have become leafless and sticky. The waxeyes are chittering. They call plaintively, *cli cli cli*.

The ngaio leaves ward off mosquitoes and sand-flies, at least the man insists on its properties. The aunts however reverted to Dimp as they gather and sat outside in the garden by the lake that never had water. The aunts show the girl how to thread the perfect intact blossoms that the ngaio drops on the ground. The aunts become nostalgic about these blossoms, how they would thread them together to make necklaces, as if she must do this too, to carry these memories forward. She imagines what they imagine. She tries to see the transient value. She imagines these small, waxy, tubular flowers, creamy with purple dots, lost and decaying, never having been made into summer necklaces, whilst in the past, sisters sat in the shade of the ngaio and talked. She wonders why the world turns wayward and instead of clement blossoms requiring careful threading, she has bright plastic flowers that clip together, small plastic tapered ends fitting into matching holes, to form a chain.

The man has already warned her that the ngaio is poisonous. It was in the book called *The Poisonous Plants of New Zealand,* which she likes to read. It describes cattle poisoned when eating it, their heads much swollen, the skin swells, breaks, dries and sloughs.

The girl sees the moon in its flowers, the moon that comes down across the ocean and kneeling upon the dunes sees the form her light creates in the shadows. The moon is struck by her own beauty. She named it her daughter and created the ngaio tree near the ocean strong with creamy flowers that drop and carpet the ground. The girl sits in the shade amongst a carpet of moon petals threading the memory of the moon's self-love.

The girl picks up the small waxeye. It's so light that the breeze almost topples it from her hands. Rain skids suddenly from the north, desultory and cool. She takes the small dead bird to the whau tree that grows near the clothesline at the south of the house. She wraps the whau leaf around its small body, encapsulating it, and lays it carefully in the corner of the doorsill of her bedroom, hidden behind the curtain where nobody notices it.

The waxeyes hang a little longer in the ngaio, flitting down to pick off insects, small caterpillars and spiders, on the edge of the toitoi that hold the bank.

The man appreciates the waxeyes. Blight birds, his father had called them, as they eat the aphids and other pesky insects. The house is still recovering from a migration of lupin caterpillars. These inconspicuous creatures began their assault upon the house in late summer. The man laid down a line of sticky poison that he had concocted himself, to protect the house. The woman was not so impressed with this experiment, as the caterpillars steadily marched through it and up the windows where they managed to excrete down the glass a purple sticky frass. Into the house they entered, through any unknown and unseen nook and cranny. Always moving south, unwavering, and once inside the carpeted, curtained home they began creating small white web cocoons in the folds of the curtains, the spines of books and in every unturned object. It became common to open books, unexpectantly breaking open the soft white cocoons. They nestled in the piano amongst the keys, inside the piano seat and the set of playing cards. They found the closet without shelves, where badminton rackets scrambled with backgammon and blunt tennis balls. They lined the bottom of all the drawers like miniature Egyptian mummies in wooden coffins. They nestled in the linen cupboard, amongst the sheets and the towels until they became the natural interstices of the house as the inhabitants accepted them and no longer even noticed them. Until the aunts visited.

The aunts when they visit liked to check the girl's bedroom. They eye critically the clothes on the floor that never fitted into the drawers, and the dust on the dresser.

The girl is careful to agree to their plans of organisation as she stands close to the doorsill, she has seen the trail of ants to the waxeye. Slowly over time all the flesh has drifted away and the structure of a tiny bird is left, feather, bone, claws and a delicate sharp beak.

Spur-winged Plover

Vanellus miles

There is an unsettled atmosphere. The sun comes up too fast. The tension is all around as if a hard beak got caught in the girl's diaphragm, and now the morning has an edge to it. There are edges everywhere; lines drawn, smiles sharp, stickiness in voices, tension in the telephone wires, a strain in the eaves. There are edges in the upright rosemary, in the sky sweeping up the sand. There is a sting in the wind and a sharp jag to the sun. Breath is something to find.

She senses the unsettled as if all that is known is now unrecognized, a warping, for in the night the house was lifted by a little finger and set down slightly askew and the doors cracked open to the west.

There are outlines of empty spaces.

She loosens her foot from its hold in the sand, the grasses quiver with leaping grasshoppers. She shuts her eyes. The spur-winged plovers whirl their rattling call. There are flocks gathering where the maize has been harvested. The birds land, eyeing her through yellow masks, walking like stocky lords amongst the yellowing shards of broken stalks, through the fence wires, horizontal boundary lines. She eyes them back, observing their sharp wing spurs protruding off their shoulders.

Blackbird

Turdus merula

The girl sits waiting for the man to come to pick her up. There is a small cement wall and she sits on it. Across the road is the school playing field. Macrocarpa and monkey puzzle trees form a line along the edge of the field. A blackbird flies down to sit next to her, peering at her with its head on one side. It hops along the ground beneath her feet. Everyone has left, all the girls with their ballet shoes put into their bags, Mrs Giles who plays the piano and Mrs Dibble the ballet teacher. Lovelock Street is quiet. The girl turns and reads the plaque on the wall, *The Country Women's Institute, Built in 1947*. In the front garden next door, a blackbird scratches untidily, uncovering soil from any debris in its search for worms and grubs. The newly planted seedlings are scratched up and thrown to the side. The bird hops, cocking its head this side and then that side.

The girl starts to peel the already peeling white paint on the cement wall. She enjoys the patterns that occur in the way the paint peels away in small pieces to reveal the raw grey bumpy cement. Her fingers encounter the soft drying moss on the top of the wall next to where she is sitting. She digs with her finger and picks off pieces of green and soil debris. She wonders for a moment how the soil got up on the wall. She swings her legs out and stretches her fingers, she half closes her eyes and looks between her fingers at the cracks in the pavement, the curb. The black bird hops under her feet back the other way. It stops by her bag, turning its black yellow-rimmed eye in her direction. The brown freckly female blackbird gives out a whimsical mellow chatter from her perch in the gardenia.

Perhaps the man has forgotten to pick the girl up. The dusk is beginning to settle, a light gloaming, a street light wavers and comes on. The male blackbird flies up to the plum tree then scatters amongst the small garden shrubs that perch on the edge of the neighbour's front lawn. It starts to call its evening alarm, a clacking, crackling fire call.

The girl makes a decision. She brings her legs downwards, drops to the pavement, picks up her bag and starts to walk along Lovelock Street towards Kope. She heads up to Landing Road, crossing by the old cemetery, cutting across the reserve to Eivers Road to get to number 83, her grandparents' house.

The shadows intermingle as she walks up the driveway; a blackbird tat tats its call in the night, a single warm light emits from the sitting room.

Red-billed Gull

Tarāpunga
Larus novaehollandiae

The girl gets lost somewhere. She doesn't know how she gets lost. It happens amongst the whispering adults. There are secrets and discussions. Appearances become warped. The "all is well" buckles like old books in the damp. Somewhere truth becomes fragmented. It slips down between the gaps in the sofa. It hangs in the dust between the cushions, with the mauve plastic strongman from the Kellogg's cornflakes packet. That's when eating becomes an anchor in the in-between places, when landing places are few. Eating became something to do whilst she looks for herself out of the corner of her eye, fiddling with the yellow plastic lion tamer. Cornflakes make a good lost food, with milk and sugar, so does butter and vegemite on Weetbix, where she finds the rare red clown. She wonders if they put strong men in every cornflakes box. Luckily there are the bird cards in the Craig's jelly packets to collect. She places the small square cards back in the box.

Being lost is a difficult business, particularly when she can't define what is lost about her. It's as if she got stretched out behind herself. Some kind of blurred ribbon which she tries to follow but there is nothing at the end of it. She is simply ill-defined, which makes her want to lie on the carpet and do jigsaw puzzles. This gives time to being found. She walks in this state of protraction and the gulls notice her. The gull is scavenger, is marauder. It opens its beak and bends down its head screaming abuse. The gull can work itself into a temper, walking around the other gulls squabbling and raucous, its whole being caught in its dispute. Always the gull knows the elongated ones, the ones with broken pieces or pieces of emptiness.

They are hunters of the discarded.

The girl wafts out behind herself, becoming accustomed to being lost, empty to the raucous calling of the gulls, dreaming into the patterned driftwood. She strays into invisible borderlands. A lone oystercatcher walks in front of her, calling out a desultory alarm call, its legs cross at an uncanny angle, and then it stops as if forgetting that she is an intruder. Two more oystercatchers land close by and give warning; they walk like grumpy old men, pissed off about being disturbed.

The red-billed gulls come screeching with excitement, diving upwards, hovering for a moment, bending back their wings before a fast descent to her head. The girl knows it is not nesting time. These ones have noticed her. She runs. They give chase before wheeling off, hovering and then landing where the sea has created a small bank of soft sand.

The girl is at the sewerage pipe. A personal landmark, the point two-thirds of the way on the walk to the spit. The sewerage comes out through a large rusting pipe. As it spews out, it creates a rivulet across the sand to the ocean. It is the same pipe that crosses the Orini canal. She sees it when she goes whitebaiting there. The pipe crosses a small sand island and then is buried under the dunes, eventually emerging at this remote part of the beach. The ocean absorbs all the waste of the town, and so it is and so it has been for years. No one bothers to think about it, because no one walks along this beach and therefore no one sees it. She has to be careful walking across it, so that her bare feet don't touch it. She usually leaps over it as it nears the ocean.

The gulls are off and up again, giving chase to a hawk that has inadvertently come into their territory. They do a full circle above the girl's head and then fly off to the town side of the river, scavenging at the back of the shops, the rubbish bins and the Heads, the name of the area where the river surges past the hills to meet the sea. The girl is nearly at the spit. She sees the town on the other side of the river. The gulls gather on the grass on the other side, already eyeing up family groups, awaiting some morsel expectantly.

This is a destination. There are bent and broken branches of macrocarpa. These fallen trees still living, grow haphazardly, their grounded tumult allows her to feel momentarily integral. She is at home and this is her river. The river smells of river. The river has the memory of forest still fresh as it backwashes, spills and eddies the muddy margins before rushing at the salty ocean. She shifts out of the place of the stranger to the place of belonging, like a swallow coming back to its nesting place.

It's time to go back, back along the mudflats, back near the raupō, back to the road in the dusk, through the tall lupins, along the pumice driveway, home with the lights now on.

The ocean is rhythmic as the wind is sleeping. The sound nestles behind the old tōtara posts, a consistent memory to the ageing of things, stalwarts to time, lichen, a pale grey-blue curling around the rusting nails. An oystercatcher disturbs itself wakeful in the horizon of the sand dunes. The night witnesses the setting first quarter moon as if waiting for the darkness to extend itself. Cattle shift, an undertone of a bellow, a moment, quiet now except for the ocean that lends itself to filling the soundscape. Through the full space of ocean, the red-billed gull calls.

Sparrow

Passer domesticus

Sparrows are gathering together. They cloister in a single tree amongst the bare branches in the winter evening. A raucous cheeping, a feast of chirping, one hundred and one cobby hang-close sparrows. One hundred and one is a good number, a well-rounded number. They have already been in the gutter, on the pavement, in the un-swept, under the shadow of awning, of roof, on the table, in the street, soft-winged presence upon the hard edges.

The girl is empty. The sparrow is not empty. It is full of chirps, a head cocked to one side, a hopping curiosity on the veranda. She is empty. Something happened. She got emptied out. She does not know what it is. Maybe if she is still enough the sparrow will hop on her arms and her chest. It will hop on her cheek and the small scratchy feet will hop on her forehead. She is the cement veranda, the terracotta pot, a stick insect, green on green, grey on grey.

The girl is at her grandparents' house. She lies on the cement veranda. She becomes as straight as she can, to imitate the Venetian blinds. Everything empty is between the lines. The fine lawn stretches to the road. The black river silt garden is cut neatly to edge the lawn, the driveway has a border of bricks, each set carefully one to another curving ever so slightly. She studies lines. She regards the cylinder metal railing that borders the veranda and the stark periphery of the jacaranda branches. The lines on the cement dissect one another to form squares. She sees if she can fit on three squares and scrunches herself to fit on two.

The girl counts all the squares and then she counts the branchlets on each branch and then she gets lost in the linear patterns repeating. She counts to one hundred and one and that starts to feel good.

The sky is evening and it's red, a red sky. Red sky at night shepherds' delight. If you step on a crack you marry a rat. Red sky in the morning shepherds' warning. Crack, you're a brat, snap.

The sparrows are roosting in the dusk. There is a chill in the air. They sort their positions, pushing margins, checking limits. It is like the tree and the sparrows are one and the tree is brimming with sparrow tears. She watches a sparrow spill outward, find its wings, pitching upwards to re-arrange and cheep, and shuffle its feathers.

The girl lies with her spine on the concrete, stretches her arms out so the dusk can touch the margins of her skin, letting fall upon the contours until the edges soften.

Dusk seeps. It is the verge she can fall through. She sees the colour bleed from the trees. The chill grazes her goose-bumped skin. Sparrows become the tree.

Chaffinch

Fringilla coelebs

Autumn entered into winter like a simple melody. The house hunkered into the dune, the easterlies swung around the ngaio that bunkered into the bank, the northerlies pushed the rain under the veranda and whipped the northwest corner. When it was out, the sun feathered the north-facing rooms. Sometimes it struck boldly before easing into the cloud covered horizon.

In the summer the girl had hung out where the dock and the sow thistles had gone to seed, watching small family groups of chaffinches. The fledglings were funny and fed lopsidedly, cheeping pathetically for the adults to feed them whilst the adults fed themselves. Now all grown up, they fly over the ground, hopping and dropping, foraging for fallen seeds, all the time heading east where the pine trees were beginning to drop their cones.

In autumn the chaffinches start congregating in groups. At a glance they are all male chaffinches, their breasts the colour of the flax flowers in spring, and their slate blue feathers on their heads disrupting the muted greys and blues of the broad landscape.

Winter is the fire, storms, books and food. Winter is the collections, gathered on windowsills and small envelopes of stamps, grouping and gathering. Winter takes space on the inside looking out.

Collecting ordered the chaotic universe. The girl collected like stringing a pattern, finding connections from one piece to another, finding a story. The chaffinch picks up a seed, and another. There is an order to things, the plant, the seed, the bird. The order in a collection of objects lies in how each is connected to another, the distinctive quality in the physical, the shape, the texture and the way each lies in contrast to another, creating its own particular aesthetic to form.

There needs to be a depository for collecting things, and this wasn't always easy to find in the girl's bedroom. The small white shelves above the bed hold the collection of bought ceramic ornaments, a Royal Doulton girl in a royal blue dress, the tip of her shoe showing delicately as if she was about to step forward to dance in a candlelit ballroom. The little blue boy on a sledge and the brown dog with the smooth back. Small and random animals, a rabbit, a hare and a little clear glass robin. In amongst these porcelain ornaments is a trajectory of information, a curious trail to peek into and then wander off. Here, a small blue dish within which she has gathered a shell of a native snail, rewarewa seeds, pieces of kauri gum, when scraped with her fingernails, she would smell and taste it turpentine scent, a very small limpet shell, also lay there, a tiny oval ring, as it top had broken off. This limpet could be the encrusted limpet, star-shaped and found at Otarawaiwere. Resting next to this dish is a round ivory coloured sand-biscuit with a single hole on the top radiating five distinct groups of two lines. Nestled next to this is the skeleton of a sea urchin, kina, imprints of stiff movable spines. In front of the sand-biscuit, a small oyster shell grown on a limpet.

She is comforted by the discovery of tiny shells as she sifts through the sand with her fingers. The tiny shells are beauty in miniature, white turrets and spiny murex, sometimes miniature sunset shells. The girl's grandmother collected shells in a random way. Her grandmother did not place them in old letter trays, grouped in Latin family names, with each name printed carefully in pencil. The girl saw this once, this carefully arranged collection, at a farmhouse out at Ohiwa. They were put on the wall in the sitting room for everyone to see. Her grandmother's collecting was like a picking up of something pretty that ended up in the caravan. The caravan was the depository of all kinds of things in the winter, a whole summer's hoarding. They eventually became lost amongst the soil of the garden or around a pot on the low cement wall of the carport. When the girl's grandmother went out to the beach she would tie a scarf around her head and wear sturdy blue shoes with a small heel and very rarely would she take them off.

The woman's feet are narrow and fine, her heels soft. The woman loves the ocean yet never needed to rush down every morning to examine any changes. The woman observes the whole interval to the sky and the open landscape. She does not need to pick up the shiny stone that the water laps like a jewel, nor does she need to take home the sunset shells with all the shades of pink and violet against the grey sand. She does however have a collection of stationery, particularly fine paper and small cards in a small box in her dresser.

Down the hall, a depository of found objects lies along the windowsills. The skeleton of a horseshoe crab that the girl's sister brought back from the States, a compact fantail's nest, skeleton leaves, and a large shell with the name Okarito the man had printed in an indelible pen. It is a list along the hallway, stories among the windowsills, small gatherings and around the corner into the kitchen is a pottery urn, the catchment for the man's collection of things that gather in his pockets. When the girl opens the lid to the urn it emits a musty smell, like the smell itself lived in the urn, mulling through and over all the objects.

The man has phases of collecting, collects whatever stamps come his way for the girl to soak in dishes of warm water. She lifts them gently off the envelopes with tweezers. She sorts them into countries and into dates. The old coins that were collected by her grandfather sat on top of the cupboard in the library. The National Geographics with their yellow spines piled on the bottom shelf in the library would sometimes call for a sorting into dates and the Everyman books all the same size would have their own cabinet in the hallway.

Every object connected to another and to another, breathing their story into the etheric. Often their story is forgotten like the black elephants with the white tusks that face each other on the book cabinet. Some collections are placed thoughtfully, or thrown into a container randomly. Sometimes they were brought for special occasions like the Irish coffee cups that sit on the dresser, fulfilling some essential purpose.

This is the comfort of aesthetics. The element that stays steady whilst the seeds are blown and discarded amongst the rhythm of the elements. The chaffinch forages for the pine seeds from the ground, pulling the seed wing out with seed attached with simple precision. Together they cluster along the branch of the pine, a winter gathering.

Thrush

Turdus philomelos

Willows in winter and a single song thrush singing a single song into the cold. The girl forgets to go where she is meant to be going, biking the stopbank, the willows and the river. She is inside home through the song the thrush sings in the white morning, drizzled gold through the bending stems of willow. The girl has gloves and a woolly hat. She is biking the stop bank to avoid the dog whose game is the girl on the bike. Once, the dog managed to bite the girl on her leg, and for a while now she has taken the slower bumpy, sandy route.

The thrush is propelling its lone, bright-edged voice into a symphony of trills and syncopated notes. Swiftly halting, as immediate as it began. In the quiet, it turns its head on the side, looking. The girl sees the layers of its soft breast, its specklety brown splotches. The girl begins to settle. She is standing. She leans into her bike. Home is here, in the smell of the river, the leafless branch, the frosted grass, the soft brown.

The thrush raises its head in one last bright call to the sky before plunging into the ground cover, becoming lost to sight in the low foliage.

Variable Oystercatcher

Tōrea pango

Haematopus unicolour

The oystercatchers' room is the shore. They are a pair, and the man suspects that they are lifelong mates. They run up and down sorting out their territory and then mooch about, randomly walking, and if they are watched a little too intensely as the man is doing now, they do a bit of strutting. When things settle to their inclination, they tuck one foot under their breast, balance on one leg and shut their eyes. The man admires their ability to sleep standing on one leg. He considers the art of napping, perhaps it's his heart that enables him to sleep in short sweet moments throughout the day. During a busy working day, he would go out to his car parked behind his shop and have a quick sleep in the back seat, or choose a chair and find that he was sleeping within minutes of closing his eyes. The wind flusters the oystercatchers' feathers. The oystercatcher opens an eye, and unperturbed anchors its body into the one leg. The man, curious, moves a little closer. The oystercatcher, without bothering to lower the other leg, hops away on its one leg, and settles in again. The man rests back. He is content right now to share the oystercatchers' room.

Someone walks along the beach with their dog. The oystercatcher flies up calling out, piercing the soft clouds piling up near the horizon. The man wakes up. He recollects himself. He has a line out with the surf caster. He has no hook or bait, he prefers it that way. He gets to sit and look with a purpose and doesn't have to kill anything. The dog owner and the dog have walked a little way ahead. They now turn back from their uncertain destination. Perhaps it was the large driftwood half sunk in the sand. The tide is in, making walking cumbersome. She stops to talk to the man about whether he has caught any fish. They talk randomly about fish and the weather. He looks wistfully at the clouds as if they have a language that they bestow upon him, and the dog owner calls her meandering dog. The dog ignores her, already up in the dunes chasing rabbits. She walks on whilst the oystercatchers circle back, crying out, before landing a few feet away, slightly miffed at being disturbed. The left-alone man stands up and reels in his line. He walks up the track to the house, with his fishing rod balanced on his shoulder.

At home, the man runs a bath, turning the hot tap on. The pump for the water supply is unreliable, it comes in spurts and starts and sometimes not at all, but most of the time the water flows gently as it has a long way to come across the paddock next door and up the hill. The bees have made their home in the pump shed. Their combs hang in layers. The door opens inward and the man, when he has to fix the pump, has to be careful not to disturb them. Once a year in the early summer the man would harvest the honey. He would get the girl to help by holding the sack open as he cuts through the honeycomb. They would both run, the man carrying the sack, and as the bees always know the thief, the chase was focused on the man.

The man is always reminded of the bees when he runs the water for the bath. The bath takes a long time to fill, and he wanders off to think about things in the library at the back of the house. It is a room that is good to think in. It still smells of Erinmore tobacco from when he smoked a pipe, and there is the musty smell from gathered things, things that settle and do not want to be disturbed. It was his time to settle into his organic chemistry books. But this time he found himself thinking about the oystercatchers. Their cry was also a signal for the other birds to protect themselves. He thought about the encroachment of their habitat from people, their motorbikes, the increase of subdivisions of the coastal sand dunes. The nests of the oystercatcher are placed just past the high tide water mark amongst the driftwood and marram grass. These nests are often unlined or sometimes he has found them with shells. He feels suddenly vulnerable and the essence of that fierce inner confidence mixed with vulnerability touches him. He feels the need to actively conserve their coastal areas. The man moves into a longer reverie of how to go about this when he is awakened by an alarm call. He wanders out into the hallway, the bathroom is situated at the end of the hall – the water now overflowing the bath, has made its way across the bathroom floor and the hallway carpet is slowly absorbing the overflow.

White-fronted Tern

Tara

Sterna striata

A rift occurs through the ordinary. Plants morph into wild beings that stretch out and grab at the girl as she bounds through the grasses and the pōhuehu. There is a shimmering force that leaks through into colour and everything vibrates and swirls outward. The container of form stops working. The girl ranges out. She looks for patterns to anchor the shimmering world. The sky is blue and eternal. The terns gather on the shore, flapping down to land, crowding and talking. The girl stops and hunkers down in the sand. The terns settle and re-settle, constantly replacing each other in the pattern of their repose, always allowing for movement in relation to one or another. The girl is aware of them but wants to watch the waves.

She has discovered that if you watch the waves long enough you uncover a pattern. Once you get it you can count the waves and predict which will be the largest. It is always the seventh wave, this followed by two more large waves and then it goes back to smaller waves until the seventh again. This rhythm holds a fascination for her. She finds her peace, the visions settle through the patterns and rhythms that she can hear and see. In music she listens to Bach. It is visual for her, sound and pattern, rhythm and pattern.

In her bedroom on each side of the door that opens onto the veranda, is a white curtain with a blue curtain to frame it. Covering the wall, the embossed faded blue wallpaper, ladies boutique, a pattern of spiral leaves with ovals and a rosebud symbol. Over and over she observes the pattern in her mind's eye, imagines her finger drawing it and practises different beginnings and different ways so she doesn't lift her finger off the imaginary page.

The terns fly up into the cirrus clouds and blue sky. They have a wing shape that can turn sharply and a beak poised to dart into the waves. The sky is blue, the terns are white, white-fronted soft greys. The bedspread is blue with white stylised flowers, and the bedside drawers are painted a sky blue with a white edge. The bedside lamp has a blue fabric pleated lampshade fastened into a wine bottle painted white with a copy of the blue pattern of the flowers on her bedspread. Matching and not matching. In the night all the blue disappears. Sometimes the white of the curtain shows up in the moonlight, and always she opens the door wide to hear the ocean.

One, two, three, four, five, six waves small, seventh wave large, eight, nine, begin again. Begin again. With her right toe she draws a curved line from left to right and joins this with her left toe to form a fish, that interlocks with the next fish, backwards and forwards along the water's edge in constant arabesque. The waves come and wash it out leaving behind oval hills with salty edges.

The spinning world has settled into its natural forms. The girl gazes up at the terns. How fast they move, their white wings so bright with grey underneath and the dark marking around their eye and head. She watches them play, skimming the water and then sitting in the water. She observes how their wings bend up and back, lifting off the water. It's difficult to keep one bird in sight as it merges with the others. There is a chaos of motion and yet it seems a synchronised chaos as if they are connected to each other, as if no single tern is working by itself but in a close weave with each other.

She wanders along the beach, forgetting time, and now the terns are wheeling above her, creating an arrow formation, a pattern of synchronized direction. Shadows form and the night is close. These terns have been wheeling and gathering as if with great purpose. They form a silhouetted arrow, and yet there seems to be no particular direction as they fly one way and then the other. There can be no more waiting to find out. As quick as she can, she runs back along the shore before it gets too late.

Black-backed Gull

Karoro
Larus dominicanus

The girl and the man are on the beach. The tide is low. The girl wanders, crisscrossing the water's edge. She looks at the patterns, the waves pressed leavings. She stares at the miniature debris stranded from the backwash, searching for the delicate, the finely carved twig softened by river and ocean, shells that encompass the whole in a cameo. She drifts. She draws in the sand with her feet, stands on the edge of the water digging in her heels, playing with the backwash. The ocean pushes a stick at her feet like a dog wanting to play. She flings it into the waves, watching the surge tug it under. There is a gleam of it rolling up behind a breaker before a tumbling pull into the eddying swell, briefly lost to sight before the foamy push to the shore. She grabs it before the ocean takes it back, and with a dancing step she flings it out again.

It is the end of the day. The man stands looking out. He contemplates the idea of fishing, at least the appearance of fishing, sitting and looking out at the ocean with a purpose appealed to him.

One black-backed gull finds a tuatua, and it flies up to a height ready to drop it, swooping down to see if the shell broke on the hard sand. The tuatua doesn't land quite right for breaking. The gull gets hold of it again, up and up it goes with the tuatua which drops a tumbling rush through the air breaking on the sand, other gulls swerve back to chase the descending tuatua, however the gull is swift in its descent. Along the beach, oblivious to the rich pickings of a tuatua, a juvenile whines and peevishly whistles to the adult black-backed gull. He puts his head down as if he is small and pathetic and near starving, persistently pestering the adult who stands erect looking out at the sea.

The clouds set out for a storm.

The evening settles, in contrast to the oncoming storm. The sky piles up brooding clouds that darken like ink falling across water. The man deliberates about the haphazard way the gulls arrive on the beach, a sense of hanging in a rest bay, playing with the edge of a storm, pressing the tattered frays of the wind. Even the young gull's peevish call doesn't seem to have enough desperation behind it to be taken seriously. The man feels like going no-where in particular. He is enjoying the shifting elements, the transitionary state of the evening sky.

The wind picks up velocity. The gulls wheel up, angling into it. Young black-backed gulls, large and graceful, spill out from the clouds, flying intimately with the burgeoning waves, lifting up and pivoting above the girl's head. The man is reminded of the mountains. He knows the extent of these gulls' flight and their love for open spaces. He has watched them sweeping the updraft at Tongariro, wild and free.

In the west, the clouds build up, leaving a line of light on the horizon. One black-backed gull rests on the sand, its back to the wind. The man begins to gather driftwood and the girl joins him. The girl bangs the pieces of driftwood she finds further up the beach, checking for sleeping katipō spiders and insects that she doesn't want to go up in flame.

The gulls start to gather and lift up, ready to go inland to hang on the wet playing fields, to check the newly ploughed fields for insects, and to come back to the beach for rich pickings after the storm.

It is nearly dark. Spatters of rain start to play with the gusts of wind. The man and the girl wind their way through the grasses and muehlenbeckia, carrying bundles of firewood. The woman has already lit the fire and so they heap their driftwood findings at the back door. The wind blusters behind them slamming the door. Coats are thrown into the washhouse. There is a sweet solidness. The girl feels the warmth inside. Soon the wind will batter the house, the rain will come in with bellowing gusts and as the waves build up and crash down, she will fall asleep to a backdrop of a thundering ocean.

In the waking light the storm reverberates around the house which sits solidly amongst the wild dune whilst the wind lashes it. The girl pulls on her clothes, throws on her oilskin coat, leaps down the dune to stand on the edge of a broken-in foredune. She stands at an angle to the salty spindrift – the clouds of spray blown from the tops of breaking waves under a driving wind. The tide is in and the waves are fearsome. The boxthorn falls down broken and pulled apart, and spinifex is dragged out in long tangled roots. Logs push and roll in the surf. The girl shields her eyes. She is part of, she is witness, she feels alone, a wild thing flung up and she feels strong standing against the wind.

The woman watches the storm buffeting the house, and checks the gardens that lie in the lee of the hill. She takes in the transient sky. She observes the different hues, the shadows, the way the storm clouds move, rapidly shifting shape and the shafts of light as the rain begins to ease. The woman watches the river roiling out of bounds, carrying with it the rich offerings of the Urewera forest, sweeping out into the ocean, showing its turbulent pathway of muddy waters.

It takes two days to begin to recede. The girl and the man walk along the beach looking at the washed-up debris, bloated porcupine fish, unusual shells, perhaps a spiny murex. The beauty of deep-sea finds. The girl finds a dead black swan, crumpled. The black-backed gulls are in flocks; the debris is their food.

The girl finds barnacles and picks them up. Her sister once showed her, after a storm, how to put the barnacles in salt water and float yeast flakes on the surface and then wait. And then something quite astonishing happens. The mantle lips of the barnacle open. Limbs emerge, fan-like, curving, then curling forward their tips to feed.

It is alive.

The girl and the man have their arms full of treasures in the slow wander back. Quiet and companionably, they cross the beach up to the house.

Harrier Hawk

Kāhu

Circus approximans

The element air is elusive if you do not know it and try to find it. Air is the chase, unstuck from the earth. The harrier hawk, kāhu, has an unusual persistence, a nucleus of sky. The wind picks up the eddies and the harrier hawk ascends. Love is like that, a rush with wind to soar and glide. Wind, air and harrier hawk until a sharp awakening into the edge of sea-gull territory and then the chase, buffeted. Buffeted, push back.

Hawk is wind. A trembling wind, a shallow wind, a fierce wind.

The harrier hawk is hunting, moving slowly, soaring, alternately gliding and flapping. It hunts rabbits and mice. It lands amongst the long grass. The beak is hooked, long legs, fair plumage. The gold of its eye imbibes, as it turns its head, the gold of the summer grass. It moves up flapping, shifting, to the wind which has called its wild companion forward silently.

Other birds chase it back. The mynas caw.

The harrier hawk lands on the tar-seal road to feed off roadkill. It lifts, flapping up against the car. The girl looks out under its soft golden plumage. The beak, the eye, the wings flapping, the car passing.

The girl is still when it comes to the hawk. A standing

stillness. She enters into a rift, a wild melancholy. In her quiet listening she rarely hears its call. She hasn't met who she will meet. She stares into hawk-wind, touching knowledge beyond her. Her dreams fall into a mute expanse, sky visions without thought, when suddenly she is chased and harried from wherever she has ventured, an inkling of an eye before it vanishes. The girl is left standing, pumice still in her hand, picked up without thought from the beach.

The harrier hawk is sweeping, slow sustained flight – patience, persistence. There is the girl in myriad perspectives, un-matching shafts, timeless. She has left persistent pathways into the wind. There is the man, standing, standing on the edge of the sand dune throwing out grass seed into the wind, and there, there is the woman. She has her arms crossed as if to say "Well yes, I know you harrier, I am of you, I have depicted your wind and your sky."

They are all there, layered up upon each other like a pen drawing overlapping. Overlapping what is in front and what is behind. The harrier lifts up, again and again.

Acknowledgements

My gratitude to Mike Johnson, for his steady support and conviction and whose advice at a crucial moment helped me to bring this book to fruition.

I would like to thank the old naturalists and ornithologists for following their curiosity, their extraordinary patience, dedication and observation: H. Guthrie-Smith, W. R. B. Oliver and M. F. Soper and my favourite; Edgar F. Stead. Special acknowledgement to the library that my parents created, the garden in the sand-dune and the wild coast of Piripai. Thanks to my writing buddy, Deb Lyttle, Cindy McGuire for her feedback as a reader, Meggan Young for her ongoing support and the Lasavia Publishing team, particularly, Rowan Sylva, Daniela Gast and Odette Singleton-Wards.

www.ingramcontent.com/pod-product-compliance
Lightning Source LLC
Chambersburg PA
CBHW031928090426
42811CB00002B/120